Sky Leaning Toward Winter

Sky Leaning Toward Winter

by Terri Niccum

MOON
TIDE PRESS

~ 2024 ~

Sky Leaning Toward Winter

Editor-in-chief
Eric Morago

Editor Emeritus
Michael Miller

Marketing Specialist
Ellen Webre

Proofreaders
Jeremy Ra

Front cover art
Zastolskiy Victor (courtesy of Shuttershock)

Author photo
Bob Niccum

Book design
Michael Wada

Moon Tide logo design
Abraham Gomez

Sky Leaning Toward Winter
is published by Moon Tide Press

Moon Tide Press
6709 Washington Ave. #9297
Whittier, CA 90608
www.moontidepress.com

FIRST EDITION

Printed in the United States of America

ISBN # 978-1-957799-26-1

Contents

To Bob, thanks for the love and understanding.
I hope Karma gives you something wonderful.

And to Amy Uyematsu,
you talk to me still through your poems.
You go on.

How to Cook a Heart

Store the organ in a cool dark spot
for up to six months. Time, after all,
is the great healer.
Dig up the muscle and rinse
until the water crimsons.
Meanwhile, in a saucepan
add lentils, something
bland enough to tame the taint.
Stir until a good consistency,
ignoring the lumps. Get involved
with the ritual of recipe. This exercise
is meant to cleanse.
Season to taste. Sprinkling mustard seeds
coarsely crushed
will yield a different mouth feel.

If this is the heart of a conqueror
overcook until tender.
If this is the heart of a loved one,
warm over a low flame; then
drizzle with prayer.
Serving feeds two, but if you're alone,
the remainder saves well
chilled in a jar strung with black lace.

Evolving

I used to measure my wealth
in paperclips,
in my ability to
keep things together,
to hold on.

Lately, I measure wealth
in the images of loved ones
who roost in me
like owls in a barn.

In my willingness
to open hands
palms up
and let what would
fly.

From the Headlines

Then there was the story
of the father in Chicago who pointed a gun
at a doctor, a guard, and two nurses and kept them
at bay so he could unplug his comatose toddler
and let that limp child
die in his arms.

When it was over –
when the little life left
had eked out of the smooth skin
that held the strand of bones –
he cried and
gave himself up to the police.

The child had swallowed a balloon
that bubbled in his trachea,
cut off his air supply, and
blocked off forever
the touch of his father's hands,
his smile, just
blocked off everything beyond
those blank little eyes.

There was no child left, really, to rescue.
But a father can't stop being a father.
So he cradled the son who couldn't
hug back, who might have slipped from his lap
as inconsequentially as a napkin, and he
fought to give that son a final death, not
that other one.

Not the death that screamed at him
every night in his dreams,
like a child with his fingers caught in the door.

La Llorona

I am the legend who lingers, the beast not caught.
Think your technology can stop me? Plug your wife's ears

and think again. Beat her deaf and keep your child away
from water, for I am the legend who lingers at water's edge,

whose appetite goes unsated, whose heart is a drowned
relic. My fingers rake the waters for sons pulled down

by my own hands. I can't resurrect mine, but I can claim
yours. I'll wrap my silver voice around your child's wrist

and tug him to me. If he sees his reflection in the lake
and looks again, he sees me. I am the treasure he'll die

reaching to grasp. I'll keep his heart in the cavern of my ribs.
I will extinguish that quick beat. Lock your wife in the house,

she can't unhear me. There is no door that can stop my voice,
and as I sing my moan, the harmonic that sticks in her head,

I plant the seed. She will finish the drowning I start.
She will hold that small head under. She will take the blame

and beg to have her hands cut off. Her loss will be as deep
as mine. And there is no lake fathomless enough to wash

away this guilt. She will cry tears that fill canyons, and then
she will stand with me, beg with me, at the shoreline

for tanned young limbs to splay waters again, for that
beaded head to surface, rend the spell with a shake,

and pull earth right with a tiny fist.

Confession

Only in harsh weather do I look for God.
But for every prayer I utter, a curse
will echo in my bones; my hands unclasp their piety to steal
anything not nailed down. Christ! the very flight of birds,
bread from a beggar, the kaleidoscopic tinkling
from a chandelier. I will lie next to you, share our breath,
swallow our vow and slip in my pocket the blue of your eyes.

Ask me for a reason, I'll say
Abracadabra! while I pick
the signature from your fingertips,
wipe the calculation from your frown. How can I explain
what I can't know myself? And honestly
(or not) the only truth I know
is the lullaby I stored in a bird's beak
for safe keeping, along with the baby's tooth.

Lazarus

On my window ledge outside, sits the cactus
I was going to throw out last summer
whenever I got around to it, but then
a freak storm flooded the patio
and broke out the succulent's green,
so it stayed. Now, I remember
to water it occasionally and
it thrives, new bright bumps
on old spines.

I once thought myself
a hothouse orchid, needing
a predetermined humidity, drooping
at the suggestion of a change
in temperature,
meting out my blossoms
to the precise and regular caress
of water, as if
their cold white form held in itself
virtue, was something
to be worshipped.
I worried myself into
a tended thing. I died more often
back then.

Years and several skins
later, I've all but become
a different species. These prickles
are good armor, this stalk hides
inner juice, weathers
dry heat and flash floods.
My roots run deeper
than I imagined, and all it takes
to bring out the green
is one good rain.

40 Days and 40 Nights

Noah, did you peek?
Or could you just tell
by the pitch of the ark,
still raining? Did you
know in advance
40 days, I mean
was there some sort of contract
so you could say to yourself
or to God
40 days, well yes,
I can endure 40 days
weathering hell because
hell had a time limit?
Were even the doves,
the olive branch, prearranged? Or
was the weary rocking
ad nauseam
the bray and squeal, mew
and puke of soft,
rough and spiny hides,
the vast rocky pummel
tap dance of hooves
of bodies righting and
re-righting themselves
incessantly falling into one another,
the stew stench of fear, urine and legs akimbo
and the indignation, the blizzard of eyes
pairs and pairs and pairs
accusing you begging you to make it stop—
was it indefinite? Nothing
you could count out on your hands?
Did you wring each of 40 days out
with your hands, clinch, unclinch
your hands and re-prop them

in prayer until,
blessed feeling,
the shaky slow standing up
in one place full moments,
a patch of solid sand
and sunlight,
the earth remaining still
long enough
for you to kiss it.

And God said *Let There Be Light*

but over the years got bored
with such an easy trick; light on
the far side of the mountain, light
on the new pile carpet, just so much frosting
on the cake. God said, *There must be more*
to life than this (even though most agreed
light was nice), rolled up his sleeves,
cleared his throat, spit

and where there had been a bland patch of light,
a happy nothing-much-ever-happens swatch of sun-stroked earth,
God poked a finger, dug a well and forced in
the unused voices of the dead. their drone
a cloud gathering, their closeted dankness
a heavy humidity, a bumping around of air,
a cleaving   until thunder tore the curtain
rain spattered
sparks   *More like it!* said God,

although the people thought he was crazy.
It was wet and cold and unpredictable. Sometimes the ache
rode their bones, and each and every one
developed a dark hollow not in their stomachs
but inside.
Still, God was seen to grin mighty,

said *Bring on the mirror, bring on the mirror!*
I'm getting bigger and darker—I grow
even as we speak—and
I want to see all of me!

Beachcomber

Three days—that's how long it has taken me
to fall in love with you from a distance.

Watching from a crevasse in this cliff as you hunt
driftwood for tonight's fire, your limbs long and knotted,

sinewy as the wood you stalk. Do we start to look like
the places we claim? Your eyes sea-misted, your long

silver hair white caps on the waves. Because, in my mind,
you have lived here for a while, time enough to recognize

which wood will feed your fire, won't smoke too much,
but flame long enough to cook your dinner, warm

your bedroll. This kind of expertise I admire,
along with your sense of purpose. I have been here

three days, watching you first from my hotel room,
then from a crack in a cliff. My only purpose to be

purposeless for three days. I am idle, but your purpose
tantalizes me. That and the way you touch wood.

You must be the lover I should have been shipwrecked
with, and we could have begun the world anew,

started from scratch. In three days you've gathered
wood enough for three fires, along with a few coins,

a small mirror and a bicycle wheel. I found only
a small round shell, one side shiny as an inner thigh—

a little moon that felt good to fondle in my pocket.
Hey, Love, tonight, when you bend to start your fire

you'll find a bottle of pinot noir I'd brought to make
the night softer and the little moon I left there before

I drove away.

What They Don't Know

I once killed a man,
a stalker, in my dreams.
He had haunted me
for days, until one night
I turned his own knife on him.

Can still feel the shank
scrunching into his chest,
my own fist with newly polished nails
driving it. Adrenalin fueled, I pushed
and twisted
until the blade stopped.

He never bothered me again.

Just a dream, but somehow
claiming that death strengthened me
for life. There is power knowing
I can kill.

I am sure most friends
think of me
as kind. I try to be.

But kindness is something
I strive for.
My real strength
is what they don't see,
what only I need to know.

I am kind to all
who are kind to me,
and to some who aren't.

But, when need arises,
I can kill.

Poof!

Last night dreaming my dream
I thought, now this is the one
I'll remember. I have forgotten
so many dreams, yet this one surely

     If our dreams are a shorthand of us
     what is erased in the forgetting?

but of course   in pausing
to remind myself to remember
I cast shadow   called
attention to myself, the watcher,
sent the dream   bright flitting bird

The Things with Feathers

These days our joy is caught
in two rosy chested finches splashing
together in a shared bath
Or in the dove that sits cooing
as water stirs around her
Or in the hawk that claims the bath as a perch
for a full 20 minutes, its gold eyes scavenging,
then – pushed by some inner compass and draped
in water, swoops up

to scale the sky

Out of Sorts

I've got a right to grumble
if the days go by like missed trains
and my heart is a cereal box
without a prize.

The same day someone told me
you can't fly without the wings
of dreams, someone else
lowered the ceiling on despair.

All day I answer a phone line of complaints
until my heart echoes, Hello, hello?
Where's my newspaper? Your newspaper
hit my cat. My paper arrived without coupons.
You must help me! Someone delivered
my life to the wrong doorstep.

I sympathize, or I offer something
that sounds like sympathy. I regret
to inform you that back copies still
cost a quarter and there is no discount
for day-old news. I regret to inform you
that I can't find that article on your cousin Harry,
and no it won't help me to hear what he looks like.
I regret to inform you that we can't print
a retraction of a retraction.
I regret to inform me
that I have stuffed my pockets with regrets
heavy as granite and that I have
waded into something called
unmitigated morass
and that I have left the phone
dangling with apologies,
like my interest, like my life
off the hook

Three Times, Three Nights

These days we take the moon
for granted.
The moon is more a place
than a thing, and we've been there,
done that.
No new illuminations
to catch like beams
in a jar. Little to carry home.

Few still dance to assure
the moon will follow
on the heels of the sun;
fewer still
call on the moon
in their efforts to move
the earth.

The moon has been reclassified,
demoted, a mundane satellite
common as a pocketbook mirror,
stripped of her power.
Someone could replace the moon
while we're not looking
with any round, shiny object.

We're too busy finding out the new,
we'd never notice.

So the stretching of our worlds
makes us poorer.
We know more,
are intimate with less.

But once a woman
with love curling like smoke inside her
could sit lonely in slate-black night
three nights—her eyes pulling down the moon,
her body drawing light like a magnet—
could find in the moon a piece of herself
and, saying a wayward man's name
three times, three nights,
could call him home.

Set Some Target

Set some target for your avarice

— William Matthews

What do I want
    kiss kiss
kiss unfeigned
one kiss neat
straight up
tossed back
means what it means
just the raw
impulse
before it means
one hot damn
unpremeditated
kiss   one
hit and run
kiss that sideswipes
one *what the?*
head-looping kiss
that leaves tongue
licking traces
like a dog
sniffing after
one dust devil
kiss that picks
you up and
puts you down
in another place

Basic Training

Start with one hand
washing the other,
a simultaneous
casting off and reclaiming,
as if all our deeds
stemmed from our hands
and water was the redeemer.

Continue with the glow of hands
after the baptism,
beneath candles or fluorescent light,
the skin we manicure
to mirror our souls,
that cloaks the deep
jet spurt.

Consider the way the bones in the hands
grow heavier
as day edges dark,
how the skin tightens
around what we've done
and not done,

how late at night
the hands would close like petals
but for the impulse to seek each other out.

Crow

It's me again,
me in a box,
my body
achingly flat,
miming walls.

Old age is
not so much old
as horizontal, and
I detest how easily
I am contained, swear
there used to be more
to me.

I crowd these walls
like smoke, clinging,
looking for the smallest
out, but
I become wall.

I never
wanted to be solid,
stable, but inertia
is a rock in the gut

and it's only
that damned crow cawing
snags my attention.

Damned lucky crow
has definition,
feathers
sound, substance.

In her brittle,
cracked song
there's homely joy.

Everything I used to reach for
she just wears
a blue-black tease—

just when I could have relented,
lived upright,
crow called

and all the miles she's pecked at my heart.

One for Woody

I've been thinking about Woody
and about how there was too much fire in his life.
How his sister burned herself to death
by lighting a match to her clothes
because her mother wouldn't let her
go to school. Then, how his father was
badly burned while tinkering with the family car.
It seems he'd been working under the Ford
and got sprayed with gasoline, and then
someone forgot and lit the spark. Some people,
even Woody's other sister, believed it was
their mother that caused that fire, the one
that burned her husband over most of his body.
Woody's mother, who lost her mind to
Huntington's Chorea, the same thing that got Woody.
And there was Woody's own five-year-old daughter, who,
one morning when he'd stepped out of the apartment
for cigarettes, found the matches he'd left behind
and set the room ablaze.
Maybe that's why Woody had to keep moving.
Maybe he felt, if he stayed too long
in any one place, fire storms consumed those he loved.
Maybe that's why he preferred jungle camps to
picket fences, places where hoboes huddled
around fires in groups, but alone, because
when your heart turns to flint
you don't take chances. Because, you know,
you can walk out to the ocean, you can
lie down on the sand, you can cry like the gulls
and kick and kick and start your own dust storm,
but all that water stretching around the world
won't be enough to put some fires out.
So you keep moving until the fever within you
catches and you can't hold your head still
or even light your own smokes, let alone
pick out tunes on the guitar, and you
watch your life burn down
like a bummed cigarette.

Mercies

Whoever unceasingly strives upward . . . him we can save.

— Goethe

Sometimes I stop striving,
I have to admit it. I take breaks,
futile ones – they give me no rest –
and only when my heart feels
like a dead mackerel.

I've even worse things to confess
if we're down to that:
Sometimes I scoff at the cloud cover
God hides in.

I say,
Cut the crap, God.
Why must I play these silly games
to find you?

Other times God sneaks up on me,
tosses the winning card
my way at the table,
plants an omnipotent
elbow in my ribs.

Like the night I stood
shivering at the corner,
my coat forgotten back at the office,
and that homeless man
with the waxed mustache and the jacket
so old you couldn't call it a color
peered down at me with concern and asked,
"Oh, aren't you cold?"

Neruda Autumnal

Do you know what the earth
meditates upon in autumn?

On brittleness, of course,
waiting to be crushed.

On the acquiescence
of trees, dropping
their yellow gold

the premeditated
sacrifice

every stalk curving
to the brown
pull

of earth
straining to catch us all
in her round basket.

Everyone knows
it is time
for falling.

What piper
but the wind
could tug so sweet?

Season's Greetings

1.
The dog in my Christmas card
has an air of expectation about him.
In fact, the whole snowy card—
very traditional with wreath-decked door and
gates, candlelit windows, smoke rising
from the chimney, and that dog
outside, sitting in the snow, patiently waiting—
the whole card seems to hold its breath.
This is the card that believes
that the dog will soon be let in
to the warmth. That somewhere
there is a hearth with a fire crackling,
something cooking in the pot,
a home for each and all.

2.
My alternative Christmas card
has two dogs—madcap golden retrievers,
huddled together in a red jalopy.
They are supposedly driving
recklessly through the snow
as if to say, *oh what the hey!*
Be merry! We got each other, we
got this truck. Let it snow, whatever.
We will find a way to cuddle through.
This is a card for those gallant folks
who, no matter what happens,
will make do.
Send it to your relatives with a good sense of humor.
Those who will find some excuse to raise a glass,
to toast and celebrate,
even in the darkest hour.

3.
My third Christmas card
is really just seasonal.
More snow; in fact in this card there are just
snow-covered trees, frost-bitten hedges
weighed down with the sodden stuff.
Snow falling through rays of light
that, although they are pretty, do not warm.
One blackbird hunched on a rickety wooden gate
and one creek frozen solid. Everything still.
Time could stop here in this whiteness.
Time might have stopped here once.
This is the card for my realist friends.
Inside it reads only, "Warm holiday wishes."
It is the card for my friends who
feel the chill beneath their wings
and squint into the blizzard.
Staunch and knowing as that bird,
they no longer ask for miracles. They will,
nevertheless, thank me for the thought.

Writing the Baby

I am writing a baby for my friend
to replace the one she lost last spring.
The one she still mourns and
will probably always mourn.
I am writing a baby to fill a space
larger than a canyon
in a petite woman.

I am waving a purple banner:
and I who could never dance
bend my knees.
Come. This is where you land
in a soft pillow place
with this waiting couple—
where the room is already painted
a hopeful pastel; once you're here awhile
you can choose your own color.

I am lighting candles again,
I who have lost my faith
still put match to wick
and say 'let it be so,'
because we are flesh
so much will be wrenched from us
but let there be

a spark stemming
to personality,
a swaddle of
limbs   wagging   possibility
to cuddle, coax
and pull
my friend
into the future.

Belated

Casket with a busted latch
crouches caddy-cornered
from mourners' view

Sole red sneaker
with crumpled toe
rides a steel rail

The mortgage extension arrives
mailbox creaking
in the dust of a moving van

My deaf neighbor sniffs
the silent open mouths
of summer roses

My blind neighbor sniffs
blown petals
of summer roses

Rain on a tractor
rusting in a field
gone to weeds

Care

I am sending you a care package,
not because you need it but
just to show I care. I'm like that,
always well-meaning but often
a day or two too late. Anyway,
in this package—imagine a polished
pine box 3x3x3 feet solid. But no,
you might not be able to lift it
once I fill it with carefree gifts.
Better make that a balsa wood box
light as a model airplane capable
of flight (yes, the airplane not the box).
But I just decided I will put that plane
in the box as part of the package,
a plane to place your best wish in.
Then climb to the top of the nearest
tall building (with the plane not the box)
and thrust that plane and your wish
Into the updraft wind, see it soar,
there, backlit by a frilly cloud,
there, imitating a red-tailed hawk
resplendent in its rise above. This
is just one thing in the box
and not even the best thing,
But you will have to wait
until you climb down from the building,
walk all the way home, lift the lid again
and look inside the box—and
until I've thought of these things—
tomorrow maybe,
to hold the rest.

Cloud Drift

1. Do you prefer hope or honey in your tea?
2. Outside the clouds conspire
3. Every day my drive demands compromise.
      In each lane speed bumps crouch
      like hedgehogs.
4. The swirl of milk like a flourish on the end
      of a letter
      to God. Oh, him again. Line busy.
5. And still the clouds, crowning touch or
      undercurrent? They can't decide...
6. Who leads who? The artist
      or the subject?
7. It would be such release to spill
8. But I can't be part of such treachery,
9. Can you?
10. One split cloud and
      the roads too wet at any speed.
11. Has your tea grown cold? Will you take a refill?
12. Oops! That was our turn. Are you tasting it yet?
13. Will you let me know
      when you do?
14. Damn old Volvo cut me off
      like an eclipse. Hell
      isn't big enough.
15. I studied meteorology in college—the only
      so called elective not filled up.
16. We learned the names of clouds but
      that evaporated.
17. If you prefer, we can continue the interview
      tomorrow.
18. Yes, I know, the clouds
      continue to bully.
19. I take my driving test in three months.
      Oh, this is your stop?
21 No worries. There's no penalty
      for not finishing the tea.

Rev!

It would be easy enough to trade
my AARP card for an aging
Vincent Black Lightning – spoked wheels
and chrome in all the right places,
a gas tank one sleek curve I'd curve into,
handlebars framing what lies ahead,
with gleaming urgency.
an engine teaching my legs
to vibrate hope, oh, antique chic
that moves with a method. With my fingers
gripping the pink slip
for that black purring beauty I could face
down this predilection to melt to still,
could hug the anger that smolders in me
like bike fumes, pull on the boots of the vagabond,
and rev, rev with the allure
of an open causeway.

The Letting

It will take a little blood.
Most things that count do.
There's more where that came from.

Make the cut deep
and wide. You will have to
let go of a lot.

Stare at the page
with the respect
the drowning show the sea.

On it you will put
rose petals and a viper's hiss.

The kiss you gave and
the one ripped from you.

The spit of the camel
you tried to pet. The cow's wet nose,
hay spackled and warm.

The first love song you shared
and who you sang with.

The brother lost to the waves
when you let go his hand
and the fingers that keep grasping,
not owning the loss.

Your dead mother,
still dead.

A lock of hair from the child
gone missing.

The echoing womb
from the babe you never had.

The lullaby you hum to soothe yourself
because you've forgotten the words,
but not the aunt who sang it.

It will take a little blood.
You will wonder
how you've held it all.

But after the letting,
you will feel like you sang
a god-filled aria in a crystal-lit hall
to a standing ovation.
You will feel like you've done that.

You haven't
but the euphoria will last
several days – will see you through
to the next time.

Magic

When I was growing up
my dad kept a hand-carved box
from India filled with coins
from around the world on his dresser.

A farm boy away from home
for the first time to fight the war,
he brought coins from every country
he set foot in back with him,

a little bit of the distant
and different tucked in a box.
Do we all romance the exotic?
Think up ways to claim it? Hoard it?

I never saw him look at those coins.
Maybe it was enough for him
to know they were there, some testament
that a boy from the smallest of small towns

had travelled elsewhere and returned
a man. I played with those coins
when I was little, built coin castles
on the bedspread before I knew

those countries' names, before I could
match countries to coins. I loved
particularly the coins with holes in them.
As if the minus gave them more worth.

I loved how they all clinked
going back in the box. Thought my dad
especially rich to have all these coins
he never put in his pocket, never

needed to spend. I didn't know then
the magic they'd made.
Dad never spoke of the war,
not until 50 years later

after we'd watched a documentary
on the boats that carried food and
medical supplies to troops. The boats
that were the most shot at and often

had no guns themselves.
That's where I was.
That's what I did in the war.

A quiet admission.
A youth of not quite 17, the Navy
had put him there probably thinking
it was a safer berth. I think he might
have looked in the box that night.

That box he'd invested with hope,
turning bad to good. Bringing these
little bits of the world home with him.
Getting home.

The Night Herons Keep Flying Toward Tomorrow's Garlands

after a line by Amy Gerstler

I want to be that steadfast. I want
that purposeful hope embedded
in my muscles, these aging muscles,
so that even in the dusk,
when my dimming eyes squint
to secure each step,
some part of me still moves toward tomorrow.
Some part of me anticipates
the opening door.

Wingspan

Lately the geese fly by before 7 each morning,
banking low, right over my window,
and cracking the dawn with fractious honking—
full of the waft of new direction.

Perhaps, they're the souls of loved one passed,
urging me, *Look up, don't fear—this*
is just another migration. No loneliness.
There will be a flock to fly with.

Join us, making a V
against a sky leaning toward winter,
seeking the right draft
to spread our wings.

Here's what I hope will happen

when it happens:
That it won't be messy.
No vomit, shit or blood
for someone else
to clean up.
I don't want that on my conscience
when I'm on my way
to somewhere else.
That it will be quick
and done
before I have a chance
to sink my claws
back into life.
Before the whatever- it- takes-
to- stay- here reflex
can kick in.
Before I take a notion to struggle
with whatever's on
the end of that line
trying to reel me in.

That no one will mourn me
in solitude. That
my friends will console each other
briefly, and then
find life too demanding
and sweet
to give me much thought.

That those who love me
will gather, read a few poems
(Not even mine!)
sing a few songs,
then meet for dinner
at a place where the food
is seasoned with forgetfulness.

That they are soon
catching up with each other,
talking future plans,
then checking their phones
and grabbing quick hugs before
hitting the road
home

where they hear their lives
calling them with unexpected urgency,
as when a mother, daydreaming,
suddenly hears the voice of her child.

About the Author

Terri Niccum's full-length collection, *The Knife Thrower's Daughter,* was released in 2022 from Moon Tide Press. She is also the author of the chapbooks *Dead Letter Box* (Moon Tide Press) and *Looking Snow in the Eye* (Finishing Line Press). A Pushcart Prize-nominated poet, Niccum was a finalist and runner-up for the 2020-2021 Steve Kowit Poetry Prize and a finalist for the Atlanta Review 2024 International Poetry Competition. Her work has appeared in *A Moon of One's Own,* an online journal from Picture Show Press; Atlanta Review; *Nimrod International Journal; Golden Streetcar; The Maine Review; Oberon Poetry;* and the *Pomona Valley Review,* among others. She is married to singer-songwriter Bob Niccum and performs with him in The Others, an eclectic musical group.

Acknowledgements

It is with deep gratitude and respect that I thank editor extraordinaire and publisher Eric Morago for finding a book in a smattering of poems, breathing life into it, and then giving it wings and a nest at *Moon Tide Press*. I only wish there was a bigger word than thanks.

But thank you, also, Eric, for pairing Zastolskiy Victor's (Shutterstock) illustration with striking fonts to create the book's tantalizingly ominous cover. You captured the soul of the poems therein; anyone who looks inside is aptly forewarned.

Thank you to Eric and Ellen Webre, Dania Alkhouli, and Shelly Holder of the Moon Tide Press team for making me feel part of a family.

Another thank you to Eric and to Nancy Lynee Woo for leading the writing workshops that sparked most of these poems. And thanks to you both for your guidance and encouragement, and for all that you do to build and nurture the poetry community. I've said it before, but again: you don't just teach writing – you teach poets how to be in the world.

Thank you to Shannon Phillips of Picture Show Press for including the poem "Three Times, Three Nights" in the premier edition of the online poetry magazine, *A Moon of One's Own*. It was an honor to have my poem placed in such celestial company.

I want to give a shout out to these individuals who have shown me the lie in the idea that writing must be a lonely endeavor. Thank you to the Salonistas and the Pterodidactyls, two writing groups whose members continually snatch me from the jaws of desperation and spur me to feast on the divine. Salonistas have in our number: Gloria Vando, Lee Rossi, Anika Paris, Nels Christianson, Florence Weinberger and Sherman Pearl. Flying with the Pterodidactyls are: Nancy Lynee Woo, Frank Kearns, Jose Enrique Medina (Henry Henry), Jeanette Kelly, and Robin Axworthy. Blessings to you all for your deep poetic insights and for the years of friendship.

Thank you to the members of Eric Morago's *Your Poem, Your Voice* and *A Poet's Aesthetic Poetry* workshops who have helped me shape and tweak many of the poems included in this book: Among these are: Alexandra Umlas, Patricia Scruggs, Elaine Mintzer, Nicelle Davis, Jeremy Ra, Aruni Wijesinghe, Nancy Beagle (Doc), Shelly Holder, Julissa Cardenas, Pankaj Khemka, MD (P.K.), Kristen Baum DeBeasi, Le Anne Hunt, Hanalena Fennel, Rosie Freed, Kathleen Goldman, and Jonathan Humanoid. I love all of your voices!

Thank you to my long-time writing pal, poet, novelist and short-story writer Margo McCall. May we continue to share our manuscripts, as well as the joys and frustrations of the writing life, forever. Yep. Nonstop. And thank you friend, neighbor, walking partner and poet I'm in awe of, Aruni Wijesinghe. Since meeting you, I've grown leagues as a writer and as a person. You have that effect on people.

Thank you to Karen Koch, a long-time friend who makes even skeptic me believe in miracles and helps me keep fun in my life.

And thanks to The Others, an eclectic vocal group who keep a song in my heart and often on my lips. Personnel include Bob Niccum, Brenda and Austin Sharp, and Carl Walls and Cathy Carroll. Thank you, Dear Friends, for letting a poet sing harmonies, bang claves and bask in your glory. And for always being game to come to my poetry readings.
Thanks to my husband, Bob Niccum, singer-songwriter, the first reader of most of my poems, and scrumptious chef, who supports and sustains me on so many levels. I could never thank you enough, so I'll just continue to harass you and die having fun.

Finally, thanks to anyone who opens this book, reads and keeps on reading. May you find a poem here that lives up to the cover!

Also Available from Moon Tide Press

Living the Sundown: A Caregiving Memoir, G. Murray Thomas (2024)
Figure Study, Kathryn de Lancellotti (2024)
Suffer for This: Love, Sex, Marriage, & Rock 'N' Roll,
    Victor D. Infante (2024)
What Blooms in the Dark, Emily J. Mundy (2024)
Fable, Bryn Wickerd (2024)
Diamond Bars 2, David A. Romero (2024)
Safe Handling, Rebecca Evans (2024)
More Jerkumstances: New & Selected Poems, Barbara Eknoian (2024)
Dissection Day, Ally McGregor (2023)
He's a Color Until He's Not, Christian Hanz Lozada (2023)
The Language of Fractions, Nicelle Davis (2023)
Paradise Anonymous, Oriana Ivy (2023)
Now You Are a Missing Person, Susan Hayden (2023)
Maze Mouth, Brian Sonia-Wallace (2023)
Tangled by Blood, Rebecca Evans (2023)
Another Way of Loving Death, Jeremy Ra (2023)
Kissing the Wound, J.D. Isip (2023)
Feed It to the River, Terhi K. Cherry (2022)
*Beat Not Beat: An Anthology of California Poets Screwing
    on the Beat and Post-Beat Tradition* (2022)
*When There Are Nine: Poems Celebrating the Life and Achievements
    of Ruth Bader Ginsburg* (2022)
The Knife Thrower's Daughter, Terri Niccum (2022)
2 Revere Place, Aruni Wijesinghe (2022)
Here Go the Knives, Kelsey Bryan-Zwick (2022)
Trumpets in the Sky, Jerry Garcia (2022)
Threnody, Donna Hilbert (2022)
A Burning Lake of Paper Suns, Ellen Webre (2021)
Instructions for an Animal Body, Kelly Gray (2021)
Head *V* Heart: New & Selected Poems, Rob Sturma (2021)
*Sh!t Men Say to Me: A Poetry Anthology in Response
    to Toxic Masculinity* (2021)
Flower Grand First, Gustavo Hernandez (2021)
Everything is Radiant Between the Hates, Rich Ferguson (2020)
When the Pain Starts: Poetry as Sequential Art, Alan Passman (2020)

This Place Could Be Haunted If I Didn't Believe in Love,
    Lincoln McElwee (2020)
Impossible Thirst, Kathryn de Lancellotti (2020)
Lullabies for End Times, Jennifer Bradpiece (2020)
Crabgrass World, Robin Axworthy (2020)
Contortionist Tongue, Dania Ayah Alkhouli (2020)
The only thing that makes sense is to grow, Scott Ferry (2020)
Dead Letter Box, Terri Niccum (2019)
Tea and Subtitles: Selected Poems 1999-2019, Michael Miller (2019)
At the Table of the Unknown, Alexandra Umlas (2019)
The Book of Rabbits, Vince Trimboli (2019)
Everything I Write Is a Love Song to the World, David McIntire (2019)
Letters to the Leader, HanaLena Fennel (2019)
Darwin's Garden, Lee Rossi (2019)
Dark Ink: A Poetry Anthology Inspired by Horror (2018)
Drop and Dazzle, Peggy Dobreer (2018)
Junkie Wife, Alexis Rhone Fancher (2018)
The Moon, My Lover, My Mother, & the Dog, Daniel McGinn (2018)
Lullaby of Teeth: An Anthology of Southern California Poetry (2017)
Angels in Seven, Michael Miller (2016)
A Likely Story, Robbi Nester (2014)
Embers on the Stairs, Ruth Bavetta (2014)
The Green of Sunset, John Brantingham (2013)
The Savagery of Bone, Timothy Matthew Perez (2013)
The Silence of Doorways, Sharon Venezio (2013)
Cosmos: An Anthology of Southern California Poetry (2012)
Straws and Shadows, Irena Praitis (2012)
In the Lake of Your Bones, Peggy Dobreer (2012)
I Was Building Up to Something, Susan Davis (2011)
Hopeless Cases, Michael Kramer (2011)
One World, Gail Newman (2011)
What We Ache For, Eric Morago (2010)
Now and Then, Lee Mallory (2009)
Pop Art: An Anthology of Southern California Poetry (2009)
In the Heaven of Never Before, Carine Topal (2008)
A Wild Region, Kate Buckley (2008)
Carving in Bone: An Anthology of Orange County Poetry (2007)
Kindness from a Dark God, Ben Trigg (2007)
A Thin Strand of Lights, Ricki Mandeville (2006)

Sleepyhead Assassins, Mindy Nettifee (2006)
Tide Pools: An Anthology of Orange County Poetry (2006)
Lost American Nights: Lyrics & Poems, Michael Ubaldini (2006)

Patrons

Moon Tide Press would like to thank the following people for their support in helping publish the finest poetry from the Southern California region. To sign up as a patron, visit www.moontidepress.com or send an email to publisher@moontidepress.com.

Anonymous
Robin Axworthy
Conner Brenner
Nicole Connolly
Bill Cushing
Susan Davis
Kristen Baum DeBeasi
Peggy Dobreer
Kate Gale
Dennis Gowans
Alexis Rhone Fancher
HanaLena Fennel
Half Off Books & Brad T. Cox
Donna Hilbert
Jim & Vicky Hoggatt
Michael Kramer
Ron Koertge & Bianca Richards
Gary Jacobelly
Ray & Christi Lacoste
Jeffery Lewis

Zachary & Tammy Locklin
Lincoln McElwee
David McIntire
José Enrique Medina
Michael Miller &
Rachanee Srisavasdi
Michelle & Robert Miller
Ronny & Richard Morago
Terri Niccum
Andrew November
Jeremy Ra
Luke & Mia Salazar
Jennifer Smith
Roger Sponder
Andrew Turner
Rex Wilder
Mariano Zaro
Wes Bryan Zwick

www.ingramcontent.com/pod-product-compliance
Lightning Source LLC
Chambersburg PA
CBHW022009100426
42736CB00041B/1407